THE LOST BOYS OF SUDAN

Lonnie Carter

BROADWAY PLAY PUBLISHING INC
New York
www.broadwayplaypublishing.com
info@broadwayplaypublishing.com

THE LOST BOYS OF SUDAN

First printing: December 2011
I S B N: 978-0-88145-443-7

Book design: Marie Donovan
Page make-up: Adobe Indesign
Typeface: Palatino
Printed and bound in the U S A

ABOUT THE AUTHOR

Lonnie Carter's plays, include THE SOVEREIGN STATE OF BOOGEDY BOOGEDY (directed by Dennis Zacek), LEMUEL (directed by Andre De Shields and Dennis Zacek, respectively), GULLIVER, CONCERTO CHICAGO (directed by Nic Dimond), THE ROMANCE OF MAGNO RUBIO (directed by Loy Arcenas and winner of eight Obies awarded in 2003), and WHEATLEY (directed by Sharon Scruggs and nominated for a Joseph Jefferson Award for Best New Work in Chicago, 2006).

They have been performed at the Yale Repertory Theater, Long Wharf Theater, the American Place Theater, La Mama, E T C, Victory Gardens Theater, Laguna Playhouse, the Carlos Bulosan Theater (Toronto), the Ma-Yi Theater Company and the Cultural Center of the Philippines in Manila under the direction of Loy Arcenas.

MAGNO RUBIO was translated into Tagalog by the poet Joi Barrios and toured the Philippines. MAGNO was performed at The Culture Project in June 2007, produced by Ma-Yi, again directed by Mr. Arcenas, as part of the first annual Asian-American Theater Festival. MAGNO then opened the Latino Theater Festival in Los Angeles at the new Los Angeles Theater Center in the Fall of 2007. In the spring of 2008, MAGNO RUBIO was performed in Honolulu at Kuma Kahua Theater. MAGNO RUBIO then went to

Romania in June and was performed in Bucharest's Odeon Theater and the Sibiu International Theater Festival at the Thalia Theater in Sibiu. It was produced by Theater Mu in Minneapolis at Mixed Blood Theater in 2009, directed by Orlando Pabotoy. MAGNO RUBIO was published in 2008 by Ma-Yi Theater Company in a volume of Asian plays called *Savage Stage*.

THE LOST BOYS OF SUDAN, commissioned by the Children's Theater Company/New Dramatists Playground Project, was performed at Children's in March 2007 in Minneapolis and directed by Artistic Director Peter Brosius. THE LOST BOYS (and now GIRL) OF SUDAN was performed at Victory Gardens Theater in March 2010, directed by Jim Corti.

CHINA CALLS was workshopped at New Dramatists, the Aurora Theater in Berkeley, Victory Gardens and The Flea in NYC.

ORGANIZING ABRAHAM LINCOLN, written with Rich Klimmer, won the Two-Headed Challenge sponsored by the Playwrights' Center in Minneapolis and the Guthrie Theater. It was directed by Brian Mertes at the Playwrights' Center and performed at Boston's Berklee School of Music for the American Federation of Teachers' Convention in 2006; then in 2008 directed by Yanna Landowne at Temple University also for the American Federation of Teachers.

Three volumes of his plays have been published by Broadway Play Publishing Inc (*Plays By Lonnie Carter*, WHEATLEY and THE ROMANCE MAGNO RUBIO).

IZ SHE IZZY OR IZ HE AIN'TZY OR IZ THEY BOTH (Yale Rep, 1970) was published by Locust Hill Press in 1985 and again by Playscripts, Inc. last year.

Lonnie is a John Simon Guggenheim Fellow and twice a Fellow of the National Endowment for the Arts, twice a Fellow of the Connecticut Commission on the Arts and a Jennie McKean Moore Fellow at The George Washington University.

He is a founding member of the Playwrights' Ensemble at Victory Gardens, now an alumnus of New Dramatists and an Alumnus Core Member of the Playwrights' Center in Minneapolis.

He teaches playwriting in the Goldberg Department of Dramatic Writing at N Y U and is a graduate of Marquette University and the Yale School of Drama.

CHARACTERS & SETTING

to be played by eight Black actors—two women, two girls, two men, two boys

in order of appearance:

AYOUN, *a cow from Sudan*

A Dinka youth who becomes A I JOSH

His FATHER

A Dinka youth who becomes T-MAC SAM

A Dinka youth who becomes K-GAR OLLIE

TWELVE, *a wizened "twelve" year old warlord*

"RELIEF WORKERS" *(They are anything but)*

GUERRILLA SOLDIER/OIL CZAR

GOVERNMENT SOLDIER/DIAMOND CZAR

COPERNICUS PTOLEMY PATRICK, *the Head Master at Camp Kakuma*

BONY-BEARDED MAN, *a bony-bearded elder*

MIRIAM MAKER, *formerly of the Southern Sudanese Parliament, administrator of Camp Kakuma*

NYANDIER, *African princess*

MOIRA MIDNIGHT, *Student Placement Counselor, mother of* MOLLY MIDNIGHT

KOOKOOROOKOO, *a Dinka young man, senior at Fargo High*

MOLLY MIDNIGHT, *senior at Fargo High and daughter of* MOIRA MIDNIGHT

ISAIAH MIDNIGHT, *basketball coach, husband of* MOIRA, *father of* MOLLY

AKINYI SMALLBONES, *a Nigerian woman, friend of* KOOKOOROOKOO

Place: Sudan and points in all directions including Fargo, North Dakota

Time: Sadly, The Eternal Present

ACT ONE

Scene One

(Sudan)

*(*AYOUN*, a cow.)*

AYOUN: My name's Ayoun
I'm a cow with a 'tude
This is Sudan
I'm your African dude
I sing of arms and the children for singing is praying
twice
and once has not worked—yet.
Children, hundreds of thousands,
too many to count, but count them we must,
conscripted for armies ignorant clashing by day
and night,
governments, guerillas, left, right,
each and every with the word Liberation in
their names
hounding, haunting, whipping and worse
We are the Cattle of Sudan,
We are proud four-footed creatures
Dinka Boys of Dinka tribe tend our herds
where and all they can
They are students, we are teachers
This is our school, out in this bush
Where boys learn to be men
We are the rule, here in this bush

For boys twelve, even eight and ten
At night ourselves are sides, our sides are pillows
We cattle rest a little in the dark, under weeping willows
We hear the sound of insects whirring, lions purring, hyenas laughing at us loudly
We're all a little frightened, in and out of sleep, but still we're feeling, feeling proudly
At dawn we move—they move us—after we've moved them awake
We scatter birds, all types of fowl, even wildebeests
We look out for the cheetahs, eyeing us, so many feasts
We have our favorite faves,
We put them forth as best; it isn't fair
Perhaps, but each one, lovely, always tries
To soothe our limbs and horns and strokes each hide
And makes us feel like we're the only one
These three soon to be called A.I. Joshua, T-Mac
Samuel, K-Gar Oliver

(A I JOSH *joins his cow,* AYOUN.)

A I JOSH:
Ayoun, my precious cow. You know today I am a man
But how I know this when I can barely shave
I've passed this dozen years, I know I can take care of you
And now we're out here in this bush alone
With twenty other boys and cows who're theirs
We're all, each tested
We're each of us in pairs
We face the days, the nights, the sun, the moon, as one
Ayoun, Ayoun, together we are joined as one.

(He falls asleep at the edge of his village, on the side of AYOUN. T-MAC SAM *is with us.)*

T-MAC SAM: I don't want to
I don't want to

I won't go into the bush
I don't want to grow up
as they say I must
I don't care about cows
Why don't they walk on their back legs as I do
In all the generations they never heard a boy about to be a man
Once utter a complaint about going to the Bush?
Hooray for them!
I set the record
Yes, I love our cows, but they will understand
Neither of us, my personal cow or me, if we stay here, will be the slightest bit disappointed
The Bush be damned!

(A MOTHER *with her daughter,* K-GAR OLLIE.*)*

MOTHER: We must disguise you, K-Gar. And send you to the bush.

K-GAR OLLIE:
For what reason, Mother? Disguise? Bush?
Let me stay here. As myself. Let the boys go to the bush.

MOTHER: For the reason to let you live
You can't stay here.
You are a girl.
That's enough to destroy you.

K-GAR OLLIE:
The Janjaweed we hear of, those camel riding genies?
Those Weeds that choke?
The Janja with their swords slicing heads and chopping arms?

MOTHER: And worse than that.

K-GAR OLLIE: Disguise me as what?

MOTHER: A boy. It's your only hope. Be with a cow.
Live as a boy.
In the savannahs. You can do it. And you must.

K-GAR OLLIE: Yes, mother. I will be as a boy. As much as I can. I will insist upon being a boy.

*(*AYOUN *guides us.)*

AYOUN: I have a premonition—I see our children so
bled-dead-tired
sleep-walking day after day
They cannot move another foot
their arms have fallen away
Hiding in the bush by day
to keep from being seen by the warplanes swooping
Running night after night
barely a step ahead of hungry animals of every sort
The Boys the Dinka Boys found us water, kept us safe
But safety's less and less these days, alas
Men are getting angry and anger doesn't pass
All of them are warriors, who worship different gods
The ones of North fight ones of South
A battle scream pours from each mouth
Children everywhere they threaten
We cows and bulls are frightened
we need some gentle pettin'
Everyone's got bad gripes and awful fears
No one says, "I'm sorry", babies are in tears
Slashed by evil progenitors crazed with greed beyond beastliness
hacking off limbs, noses and ears
shoving the barrels of rifles up every opening
the tiniest bodies never knew they had
mothers with child disemboweled by crazed canker-cocked
dingleberry-dicked lupine losers

And for what? Oil, diamonds, cobalt, magnesium, all the precious minerals
and unobtainia that will never re-generate, once gone, all gone
Get them while you can, at whatever cost to life and love
destroying both, with not enough sand in the
Sahara to dry up all this blood
What will happen to us
if these boys no longer tend us?

*(*A I JOSH *asleep on the side of* AYOUN. *His* FATHER *approaches and speaks over him.)*

FATHER: My son, I have been given a choice
The rebels say you have betrayed them to the government
They say I must kill you or they will kill our entire family
They will not kill you
They say I must do the deed
kill my son
and break the cycle of violence
I do not understand how this breaks the cycle

*(*FATHER *pulls a knife. He hesitates and is struck and falls. His falling wakes* A I JOSH.*)*

A I JOSH: Father—

*(*TWELVE, *a wizened twelve year old, guerilla mufti, the obligatory AK-47, appears.)*

TWELVE: I am Twelve, here to protect you
Wise Twelve years bold, this gun makes me old
He was about to kill you, little one
He had his orders, and not with a gun
But with this knife he would have slit your throat
As if you were some sacrificial goat

A I JOSH: My father wouldn't raise his hand to me

TWELVE: Little Man
Slit your father's throat.
He's now the sacrificial goat.

A I JOSH: No. He cannot die.
He's raising me to head the family
Mother, sisters, uncles, aunts and Grandma
    living in peace on this land
    taking your hand, Pa
I won't let them lie about you

TWELVE: Twelve will show what's false and what's true
(He turns on a mini-tape recorder.)

FATHER'S VOICE: They will not kill you
They say I must do the deed
    kill my son

(TWELVE clicks off the recorder.)

TWELVE:
Now, Little Man, Twelve gives you the same choice.

A I JOSH: It was a trick and not my father's voice,
    an echo, a sound from the sky
    twisting his words, he cannot die

TWELVE: No matter, little one, your treachery is real
You told the government, on the run
That Twelve would be moving south
Now Twelve's here to smash your mouth
My bodyguards will hold you down

A I JOSH: I never spoke to anyone.
And where are your bodyguards?

TWELVE: What—I turn back fire, swallow bullets whole,
my guards will attest?
I cannot be contained. Where—

A I JOSH: —are they? They've abandoned you.
Now I'm the father, no longer the son. What are you
going to do?

TWELVE: I cannot be abandoned. I am Twelve

A I JOSH: And have been for many years, I think.

TWELVE: I'll teach you a bloody lesson
I'll Torch your huts
Waste your herds
Kill your girls
Emasculate your boys
Leave your skeletons for someone's toys
Leave your parents for vulture birds
Blow your village all to bits
We are the Revolution
The Twelve Year Old Solution
Right, my honies?, my sisters, my guards?
Stand not on the order of your coming
Let's hear it for Twelve!

(Explosion. Firestorm. Conflagration of village.
Enter on steed, a GOVERNMENT SOLDIER. *Speaks to* T-MAC SAM)

GOVERNMENT SOLDIER:
This village is being swept of rebel scum
We all know where they come from

(A REBEL SOLDIER *rushes on.)*

REBEL SOLDIER: Come from The Lord of the Peoples' Liberation Front for a United Front!

GOVERNMENT SOLDIER: Dare attack the Democratic Liberation's Back for a United Back and we'll rip apart your Front!

T-MAC SAM:
I want no part of your Lord or his Back or His Front
Rip out each other's fronts and backs
I want no part of your murderous hunt

(The SOLDIERS *fight.)*

REBEL SOLDIER: Government Scum.

GOVERNMENT SOLDIER: Rebel Swine.

REBEL SOLDIER:
Poisonous bunch-backed Government Toad.

GOVERNMENT SOLDIER:
Quintessence of canker-blossom Rebel Slug.

REBEL SOLDIER: You Rampallian.

GOVERNMENT SOLDIER: You Fustillarian.

REBEL SOLDIER: Roast meat for worms.

GOVERNMENT SOLDIER: Elvish-marked, abortive rooting hog.

REBEL SOLDIER: Variest varlet that ever chewed with a tooth.

BOTH: Thou art a boil a plague sore/ infinite and endless liar/ an hourly promise breaker
You bolting hutch of beastliness.

(They wrestle each other off to their deaths.)

(More Explosion. More Firestorm. More Conflagration of village.)

*(*K-GAR OLLIE *rushes on.)*

K-GAR OLLIE: Mother, I can't protect you from that boy. Leave her alone!

*(*K-GAR OLLIE *is discovered over her ruined* MOTHER. *She speaks out to the Boy/Man who raped her mother.)*

K-GAR OLLIE:
My mother you got away from, young man
After you had had your way with her, young man
You left her there to shudder in the dust
And then you moved away feeling you were just
You pulled her hair, you bit her neck, she cried
You needed this release, you'd been out in the bush
For months and years, you'd been so shoved and pushed

And so you seized my mother to prove you weren't
NO THING
And that your life was worth its starving weight, that
you were SOMETHING
You "liberated" her, you lonely boy
You slapped her right and left,
you played with her as if she were a toy
And then the elephants took you off to hell
You just had poached a nursing mother's tusks
You were a child like me
Despite what you have done, I pity your soul

(Suddenly an elephant rampage has found them.)

T-MAC SAM: So, you're a poacher, you are
Let's be clear what that means
You murder elephants,
then you saw off their tusks
Or, worse yet, you pour acid where the tusk meets the
hide
Then yank out the ivory, leaving holes charred
all the way inside the carcass
which you leave to fry in the broiling sun

K-GAR OLLIE: And you do this, elephant after elephant,
the earth strewn with your poaching,
like eggs poached, scorched, fried, broiled,
elephant flattened after elephant,
sometimes you don't even bother to murder,
you merely use your stun guns,
do your dirty work and leave a maimed
elephant
to awake to a tuskless fate

A I JOSH: Well, you won't stun my personal cow Ayoun
you won't yank out her horns
Get out of my country
and get out quick
Your ways and your means

have made me quite sick
And when sick gets serious
no matter how delirious
Sick fights back

(Our three youths, bled-dead tired have come separately to a stream. This is the first time they will have seen each other. Much adlibbing as they awake and drink from the stream—Who are you? Are you yet another enemy? No. How can I trust you? What is my fate?)

THE THREE: What is my fate?

A I JOSH: Not so fast—or we'll have no fate to seize
We appear to be alike and we have no guns

T-MAC SAM: We're all very thirsty and hungry

K-GAR OLLIE: And chased. We've all been chased, would be my guess. Isn't that right?

A I JOSH: Right as rain.

T-MAC SAM: Or water.

A I JOSH & T-MAC SAM: Or food!

A I JOSH: Let's think this through—

T-MAC SAM: I need to eat this through—

K-GAR OLLIE: I'd like to know why we—

A I JOSH: —don't set up camp beside some stream and stay—

T-MAC SAM: —and try to grow some food and have a life—

K-GAR OLLIE: —it's not too much to ask or is it now? What tribe are you?

T-MAC SAM: And what's your religion?

A I JOSH: What does it matter? I'm from the Upper Country. I have my gods.

T-MAC SAM: And so do I. My gods are from the Middle Country where I am from.

K-GAR OLLIE: I have a god whose face I keep around my neck.

T-MAC SAM: I don't see your god.

K-GAR OLLIE: Around my neck.

A I JOSH: I don't see your god.

K-GAR OLLIE *(Feeling at her neck)* My god is gone.

A I JOSH: I keep my god in my heart.

K-GAR OLLIE: I don't see your god.

A I JOSH: That's because my god's inside me.

T-MAC SAM: I want to see your god.

A I JOSH: I feel my god.

K-GAR OLLIE: Let me feel your God.

A I JOSH: I can't just let you feel inside me.

K-GAR OLLIE: You could see and feel my god—if I still had my God.

A I JOSH: I can't just open myself up.

K-GAR OLLIE & T-MAC SAM: Why not?

A I JOSH: Because my god doesn't like to be looked at.

K-GAR OLLIE:
My god likes—liked—to be looked at at all times.
I wonder who's looking at my God now.
What tribe are you?

A I JOSH & T-MAC SAM: Dinka.

K-GAR OLLIE: Dinka?

A I JOSH: Yes.

T-MAC SAM: Yes.

K-GAR OLLIE: You speak a little—strange.

A I JOSH: What's strange?

T-MAC SAM: Strange?

K-GAR OLLIE: I am Dinka.

A I JOSH & T-MAC SAM: You are Dinka?

A I JOSH: You speak—

T-MAC SAM: Strange.

A I JOSH: If we are all Dinka, we must be from different parts—that is why we speak differently, one from the other.

K-GAR OLLIE: But then we all have the same gods.
So your god inside is my god on my neck.

A I JOSH: So you don't have to see your God, because
you see your God-
that is, around your neck
and I can see my God too
and feel my God because my God's inside

T-MAC SAM: Who's my god? I thought I knew. My god's in the sky behind that cloud.
Are you sure we're all Dinka?
I know I am—Middle Country.

K-GAR OLLIE: Lower Country.

A I JOSH: Upper Country.

THE BOYS: AND ALL DINKA!

K-GAR OLLIE: —it's not too much to ask or is it now?

A I JOSH: No, it's not. It's just what we must be doing.
Upper, Middle, Lower

K-GAR OLLIE: —join together

T-MAC SAM: With gods inside out and outside in
and behind—that cloud is gone

A I JOSH: There are some fish in this stream and I'm going to catch me one.

K-GAR OLLIE: Catch and cook.

T-MAC SAM: Or eat one now.

K-GAR OLLIE: Raw fish? You Middle Country Dinkas—

A I JOSH: I'm seizing a fish.

K-GAR OLLIE: Dinner will be served!

T-MAC SAM: AHA!

A I JOSH: It's not too much to ask now, is it?
To make—to have a life?

(As the three exult and dance, AYOUN *steps forward.)*

AYOUN: These Boys are only beginning a journey—this is its start
There is a camp called Kakuma
And there there's a measure of Peace.
It's for children like ours
But it will take a thousand million steps to get there.

(Tracer fire. An all-out attack. "RELIEF WORKERS" *rush on)*

"RELIEF WORKERS":
We are your friends. We're gonna put you to work.
We're here to take you to the oil fields.
We're here to assist you
What are your names?
What are your names and whom are you protecting
while we are protecting you?
Hey? Speak up! Hey?

A I JOSH: I –I'm a—I—I'm a—I

"RELIEF WORKERS":
A I, Are you—speak up, O K? Hey?

A I JOSH: *(Terrified)*
A I. Hey?? —who are you protecting us from?

"RELIEF WORKERS": Enemies of the State—A I Hey

A I JOSH: The State—of what?

"RELIEF WORKERS": The State of the State—we'll call you A I Joshua Hey?, after my brother's middle name. You, second boy, what is your name?

T-MAC SAM: Don't—Don'—Don'—T-t-t-t-t—Smack me—T—Smack me—don't smack me!

"RELIEF WORKERS":
We won't hurt you, smack you upside the head
Not a chance, we'd rather leave our own selves for dead
Trust us, we bring you relief, keep you out of harm's way
What you get in return, a spot of work in the oil fields it's almost like play.
So, T-Mac, we never 'mack you
We'll call you T-Mac Sam, after my cousin's middle
And you, Third Boy, who are you and what is your name, O K?

K-GAR OLLIE: O K, K—K-k-k-k-k-

"RELIEF WORKERS": K? Great. K-Great, we'll call you K-Great Ollie, my uncle's middle.
We really must bring you into the modern world.
Forward, march!

*(Time has passed. The three have marched for several hours. The "*RELIEF WORKERS*" are high and drunk)*

"RELIEF WORKERS":
Yes, my lads, a spot of rum n' runnin'
To the Pump
What could be better, shootin' n' funnin'
To the Pump
Let's hear it for the oil from the soil, let's not be late!
Here we are—At the fields.
On to the Pump
You set the drills below the earth
The oil pours forth for all it's worth

And on to the pump
And you'll pay us at the pump.

(The oil wells burst forth and drench our heroes.)

(The "RELIEF WORKERS" *sing to the tune of* O, I wish I was in the Land of Dixie.*)*

"RELIEF WORKERS": O, I drill it, love, in the Land of Oil
Sticky wet from boiling soil
Pump away Pump away Pump away Gasoline
In Oil Land where I was born in
Early on one boilin' mornin'
Pump away pump away pump away, gasoline
O, I'm joy'll I'm in Oil/hooray hooray
In Oil Land I'll take my stand
To live and die in Oil
Away away away /down Gasolina

*(The oil wells explode. Who has set them on fire? Only The Shadow knows. The three escape the fire, but are stopped by yet another marauder/*GUERILLA, *this time with an African-Gallic accent.)*

GUERILLA:
Hey, *mes garcons,* you're just the ticket, *Mais Oui!*
To fight the South you need the North so bads
Protection's what we offer you, you see?
We need you much as you need us, you lads
Please take this gun and pump them up like this
Get set to shoot when I tell you
The enemy is everywhere, snakes hiss
Snakes always take the form of South'ners too
Now leave your older ways, we'll show you fame
You've never had such glory, that's the name
Of what we're fighting for, it's why we chance
Just ev'rything, we've nothing but this dance

*(*K-GAR OLLIE *takes the offered gun.)*

K-GAR OLLIE: Let me see this—what's it called?

GUERILLA: A-K 47 or Kalashnikov.

K-GAR OLLIE: How you pump it—just like this?

GUERILLA: You feel it and now you're better off.

K-GAR OLLIE: I'll join and so will my new brothers.

T-MAC SAM: No, I won't. It's crazy.

K-GAR OLLIE: Feel it, it gives you power.

A I JOSH & T-MAC SAM: Over what?

K-GAR OLLIE: Over this.

GUERILLA:
A little joke, little man, you'll make a good Guerrilla.

K-GAR OLLIE: No joke, it's already pumped
A K or Kalash, run now, big man has been dumped.

T-MAC SAM: We'll join our brother now.

A I JOSH: Go—Rilla, boom boom POW

(GUERILLA *rushes off.)*

T-MAC SAM: K-Gar, that was great

A I JOSH: Really good, K.

K-GAR OLLIE:
It's the gun, it makes me feel so—FRIGHTENED!

THE THREE: We see them all—we must takeoff, escape
These Go—Rillas, they take the strangest shape

K-GAR OLLIE:
I see them everywhere—they're stalking boys
These soldiers who would take our lives away
We must move fast, escape this war and then
We've got to get to Camp Kakuma, what's there?

A I JOSH: I fear I hope I hope I fear that there's
The answer to our needs, but what'll we do
If there's danger there and awful jungle noise

THE THREE: O, cattle dearest, we're so far away
we miss you, miss you. We just want to play.

*(*AYOUN *appears.)*

AYOUN: And so our youth trudged and crawled and
marched and ran across the bush,
dodging bullets, foraging for roots and the
sometime berry, aiming their way to—Kakuma
And even if they could have gone as straight as a
Masai spear
The armies, krypto armies, pseudo armies, would have
stopped them in their tracks.
And so they were conscripted by every remnant of
every colonial power.

K-GAR OLLIE: What is "colonial"?

AYOUN: "Colonial" is when someone who is not from where you are comes to where you are and tells you what to do and say and think.

T-MAC SAM: I do not like that.

AYOUN: "Colonial" is someone coming to where you are and taking what is yours and telling you you better like it.

A I JOSH: That is something I do not like.

AYOUN: "Colonial" is someone coming to where you are and forcing you to work for them and taking all the things you make.

THE THREE: That is all the things we do not like!

AYOUN: But for this moment, this precious fleeting moment, you have may breathe before the next invasion takes you away.

A I JOSH: So let us form a camp so we may better protect ourselves.

T-MAC SAM: Let us cook a meal so that we may better fill our hungry selves.

(Lentils Onions Rice rouses K-GAR OLLIE *and she takes the lead on this song.)*

THE THREE: If only we had lentils, onions, rice
We'd have a lovely meal, o so nice
We'd put them in a pot and boil them, boil them hot
If we had a pot
If only we had lentils, onions, rice
If only we had spices and an herb
These roots, these flowers, weeds would taste Soup-Perb
If only we had lentils, onions, rice
How sweet to be our tongues,
when tasting something
O so nice
If only we had lentils, onions, rice
AND A POT!

*(*TWELVE*, barely recognizable, in green smock and green plastic slippers stumbles on, a large battery atop her head.)*

TWELVE: I am the radio operator's assistant. Have you seen him?

A I JOSH: Radio oper—what? You're Twelve.

TWELVE: All you need to do is plug me in. I have to get the message back.

*(*TWELVE *puts down the battery, sits and empties her shoe of blood.)*

T-MAC SAM: You have put this thing upon the ground, Twelve—

K-GAR OLLIE: And your shoe is full of blood, Twelve.

TWELVE: Invincible am I, Twelve to the death
I stop bullets with my mouth and grip them in my teeth
Tanks cannot crush me, I climb upon them and keep them beneath
Eternal infernal, give me my crystal meth

K-GAR OLLIE: Twelve, you have no help, put aside
these thoughts
Stay with us—

A I JOSH & T-MAC SAM: K-Gar, stop!

K-GAR OLLIE: She's a youth like us.

A I JOSH: Long stripped of youth

T-MAC SAM: Gone and forgotten.

TWELVE: *(With firm resolve)*
I must back on my shoe put
No blood no more coat my foot

(TWELVE puts the shoe back on, the battery back on her head and starts to exit.)

TWELVE: I have to get the message back. I am the Radio Operator's Assistant. Have you seen him? Just plug me in.
(She is gone.)

A I JOSH: K-Gar, Twelve would have had me kill my father.

T-MAC SAM: K-Gar, Twelve's vicious and beyond hope

K-GAR OLLIE: Twelve's not beyond and I'm not sorry.

THE THREE: And suddenly we had to leave this makeshift camp

K-GAR OLLIE: Boys by the tens, hundreds pouring forth
War in Ethiopia like Sudan before it
Soldiers driving us into Kenya south

A I JOSH: Pushed to cross the Gilo River
Bullets behind us, skipping about us
Crocodiles snapping the surface ahead and beneath
Barely above the water was a bridge of swaying rope
We dozens hundreds clinging to each other without
hope
Our tongues twisting in and out our lips

blood across our teeth
Crocs, bullets, bullets, crocs

T-MAC SAM: The crocodile has a toothsome smile
He opens his mouth for all to see
He shuts his mouth with you inside
Your arm, your leg goes for a ride
And all that's left for you to be
Are stumps, your trunk, a little pile

A I JOSH: One boy grabbed my foot he would not let go
On the bridge swaying splashing all my brains were in my foot
I shook I shook him off he grabbed again
I hobbled forward dragging him along
My foot my foot I had to have my foot
Let go! I NEED MY FOOT!
And then he was gone and I could move
My chest hurt I couldn't catch my breath
My foot felt for him I couldn't look my foot looked my foot couldn't find him
I didn't even hear him cry
Now I hear him cry
Now I hear him cry

(Camp Kakuma The City Of Children)

(COPERNICUS PTOLEMY PATRICK *enters.)*COPERNICUS:
Boys hundreds thousands exhausted out of their skulls came to Camp Kakuma
They tripped slipped upon the dust the mud and fell to the ground
some wearing little cloths around their middles and nothing more.
One boy with a jaunty hat came with nothing else and did not seem to mind
nor did the others
Another I recall kept flailing and rolling on the sand and pebbles

and kept jolting up as if he'd had this hideous nightmare
and kept screaming at the other boys to keep on singing,
even though no one was singing
They lose their culture when they are driven so hard
So many lost to cholera and all manner of airborne disease
They are mad and dangerous to themselves
and you hope you hope they will pass out
so that you can move them a bit
and stroke their foreheads with a damp cloth
Then when they finally do, they either sleep fitfully
or still like a stone so much that they appear dead
And some of them are
When the others awake, we give them broth, a little meat,
gristle really, to try to build their strength
They are suprisingly strong, or at least resilient
and in a few days they, some of them, even get a bit cheery
Others remain delirious
The boy who insisted upon the singing now just stares ahead
I am not hopeful he will come around.
Today is the first day of class.
Yes, there is an attempt at schooling.
I am Copernicus Ptolemy Patrick, head Master.
Good morning, class. You may say "Good Morning" back

THE THREE: Good morning
Back
Good morning back

COPERNICUS: I see. Just three of you today. Well, we have to begin somewhere. What are your names?

A I JOSH: A I Josh.

COPERNICUS: What does the A.I. stand for?

A I JOSH: What does the A I stand for.
Stand for.

COPERNICUS: I see. And you?

T-MAC SAM: T. Mac Sam.

COPERNICUS: The "T" stands for—

T-MAC SAM: T.

COPERNICUS: And the Mac stands for—Mac. Alright, Sam. You, young man?

K-GAR OLLIE: K-Gar, stands for Kevin Garnett.

COPERNICUS: Who's he?

K-GAR OLLIE: I don't know.

COPERNICUS: Do you know your numbers?

A I JOSH: *Un Deux Trois Cinq Quatre*

COPERNICUS: One two three five four. *Parlez francais vous?* O K, that can be worked with. The alphabet?

T-MAC SAM: Soup.

K-GAR OLLIE: *(Singing)*
Next time won't you sing with me?

COPERNICUS: One more—T-Mac? Do you know the planets?

T-MAC SAM: Pluto is Mickey's dog.

COPERNICUS: Who's Mickey?

T-MAC SAM: I don't know.

COPERNICUS: How is it that you know these snippets? Where do you pick these things up? And how will we ever fill in the gaps?
(He speaks to the audience.)
The youngsters worked very hard and although their

progress was slow, it was steady and in no time, well, years, really, they began to sound rather like—me.

A I JOSH: Mister Copernicus Ptolemy Patrick, explain your name Copernicus to us. What, pray tell, does it stand for?

COPERNICUS: You explain it to me.

A I JOSH: He was a man who reversed the Ptolemaic system. Now explain to us who Ptolemy was?

COPERNICUS: Alright, I shall, seeing as how I think you're all bluffing—he was a man of ancient times—

T-MAC SAM: He devised a system of the universe which had the earth at its center, with man at the center of the earth.

THE THREE: Brilliant, my dear man, you have an excellent future ahead of you rotting right here at Camp Kakuma.

COPERNICUS: *(To the audience)* The boys had a point, a painful one. The longer that they stayed at Kakuma, the more they learned—up to a point. In fact, they stopped learning because they ceased to see the point. When one war was supposedly over—

*(*TWELVE *rushes on.)*

TWELVE: The war is over! It's time to call it a day! DAY!
Let's all return to our hearth and home
    'cept no home and hearth exists
Let's stay right here at Kakuma Camp

*(*TWELVE *hesitates, then rushes off.)*

COPERNICUS: *(To audience)*
With that war supposedly over, another flared up right where the last had flared down.
But there was movement of a positive nature from across the seas

Finally someone was beginning to pay attention to those of us on The Dark Continent.

(COPERNICUS *addresses the three.)*

There's been a new development.

K-GAR OLLIE: What's a "development"?)

COPERNICUS: It has to do with settlement.

T-MAC SAM: And what the Hey is settlement?

COPERNICUS: It's when you're moved to safer places.

A I JOSH: Moved where?

COPERNICUS: To America.

T-MAC SAM: To A-M-E-R-I-C-A?)

COPERNICUS: Chicago, Massachusetts—

K-GAR OLLIE: That's where I want to go—Massa—Choo choo where the trains are—

A I JOSH: Chicago where the bulls are. I have read about this, where there are a lot of bulls.

COPERNICUS: Minny—Soda—where the tiny soft drinks are.

K-GAR OLLIE: Minny—Soda, what is that?

COPERNICUS: Where very light bright people with down upon their faces speak in strange high-pitched sing-song tongues.

K-GAR OLLIE: I don't want to go there. I have my own high pitch and I am from the South where I want to stay.

COPERNICUS: And Fargo.

T-MAC SAM: Far Go? Go Far? How far far go?

COPERNICUS: Very farther than Kenya. No—Fargo is the name of a city.

K-GAR OLLIE: And how to get there? Why would we go to all these places?
And who wants to take us there?)

COPERNICUS:
Lutherans, Catholics—with a mission to save
Or at least give the chance, to be not a slave

(COPERNICUS recedes and the three are left alone. They sing a trio, a little of African Mills Brothers.)

K-GAR OLLIE:
Who are these Catho-licks and these Luther Anns
And what have they in mind for us, we fear

A I JOSH: They have some plans, these Luther Anns, their god's
We'd work for them and herd their cows with sticks, and prods

T-MAC SAM:
And what of Catho-licks who now abound
What if they want to take our souls and run
why can't we have some fun
Just sitting in the sun

THE THREE:
We're children, wanting all the wholes, the parts
You Catho-licks, you Luther Anns, your names
You drive us crazy, crazy with your games

COPERNICUS: They're not games. All of us here in Kakuma under this tree I call a "school,"
we don't pretend to think we're saving lives.
We only do a bit. We try to do our bit. Our little bit.
This tiny itsy bitsy spider bit.
We're climbing up a waterspout and the drain is pouring out
and we the itsy bitsy spider climbs up the spout again.

T-MAC SAM: And so these years have passed, so many
threats we've spared you,
but we children were not spared
Lions seizing us at the edges, terror always there
and those particular times we cannot erase
always ever in our face

A I JOSH: So hideous were the faces
that confronted us in the tiniest space
pounding loud, grounding into dust
worse than lions, holding apart one leg, then the
other

K-GAR OLLIE: Must man be this way?
Must man, six of them,
Must man be this way?
grinding, minding nothing that speaks of
gentleness
All that shouts—Tenderness be gone!

ALL: Love, you have no place
This is not the human race

COPERNICUS: This too somehow passed
And we moved on,
not as though the awfulness had not occurred
But that we knew we could do no other
be no other
We still had breath
And the development, the settlement was now in full
debate

(The elders of the tribe just say no.)

*(*MIRIAM MAKER *enters.)*

MIRIAM MAKER:
We're sending you off but we won't lose you
We'll follow your progress and if you choose, you
Can be our leaders of the southern Sudanese
We're sorely short of leaders, tyrants have them on

their knees
We're asking you politely when really what we mean
Is you have an obligation to save a wretched teen
So go away and get your education proper
But we know that when you can return you must
Our many men who work the manganese and copper
Deserve your generosity, you now have all their trust
Some warnings few when in the USA
You'll be few boys inside of thousands
Men and ladies looking straight ahead
they cannot be, they seem
Glass buildings, bright lights, like you never fantasize
Don't go and be attracted by all the play/ whatever
they tell you, it's lies
Don't drink the beer, it's new to you
You'll burp like not before
There's something called 'Fast Food and Drink, All-
You-Can-Eat,' –
What a concept! —you'll slurp while craving more
And sweet things 'Skittles' that they call
What they are, after all, I cannot tell at all
Just keep your wits about you when you dream
The thing you want the most is never what it seem

(BONY BEARDED MAN *bursts upon the scene.)*

BONY BEARDED MAN:
Don't go at all, black boys
There are many Negroes in those States
Don't think you know them because of their hair
They're not like us
They sprinkle smelly things upon themselves
They put these smelly things underneath their arms
And then they rub them there and in their crotch
They rub their behinds' cracks with white things made
from trees
Then they throw these white things down white holes
And water rushes them away

They are barbarians who have pulled up their African
roots
And left them to rot in the sun
They would spoil the earth
They are not from here, they are not from there

MIRIAM MAKER: Who are you that you know so much?

BONY BEARDED MAN: I was here before the savannahs; I am as ancient as the bush. The oldest elephant was a mere cub holding on to the tail of its mother as I strode these patches of scrub and rode the backs of the Kings of the Jungle. Who are you?

MIRIAM MAKER: I am Miriam Maker, formerly of the Southern Sudanese Parliament, sent here to administer this camp.

BONY BEARDED MAN: I know that the Southern Sudanese Parliament no longer exists.

MIRIAM MAKER: You're telling me, Bony Bearded Man, o you, as older than these savannahs, you who strode this scrub and rode the backs of rhinoceri through the terrifying horrificating jackal-packed, evil-spirited, black mamba infested waters of death, o you Proud One, do you know the terrible injustice in and of these camps?

BONY BEARDED MAN: I know what I need to know. And there across the seas and through the airs above, these boys must not go.

MIRIAM MAKER: Among these boys may be the future President of Southern Sudan.

BONY BEARDED MAN: There will be no Southern Sudan. It will all be destroyed by this war between those that smell one way, and those who smell the other.

MIRIAM MAKER: These boys are too precious to be left behind. That's just the way it is. Few are chosen, and many are left behind.

BONY BEARDED MAN: And will these few return?

MIRIAM MAKER: I do not know. I do know that there is a law and that here there is no law

BONY BEARDED MAN: And if they do, will they be corrupt? Will they be common thieves?

MIRIAM MAKER: I do not know. I *do* know that they are going to a land where they cannot just come and kill you.

BONY BEARDED MAN: And what of women who will tempt them so, with their tempting ways and their tempting dress?

MIRIAM MAKER: They have seen all the tempting dress and undress in the world. The women in the bush—what do they wear? Next to nothing.

BONY BEARDED MAN: You have been in the world?

MIRIAM MAKER: I have been in the world and I have imagined all the rest.

BONY BEARDED MAN: They will come back, if they do, and they will bring revolution.

MIRIAM MAKER: True revolution. That is what I hope. These boys are off to a better life so that they might return and help us all to a better life.

BONY BEARDED MAN: Isn't it pretty to think so?
(He exits.)

MIRIAM MAKER: *(Speaking to the three)*
Tomorrow when you're on the plane and traveling to
 the West
You'll have been farther through the skies
Than any of your forbears ever dreamed that they
 would be
You'll be crossing oceans vast, 'though you've never
 seen the sea
A year will pass like nothing—at its end

You'll wonder why we didn't sooner send you
You had a secret that I know my dear.
But not to worry have no fear.

(The march to the plane of A I JOSH, K-GAR OLLIE *and* T-MAC SAM.*)*

A I JOSH: The airplane's here. Let's march.

T-MAC SAM: It will come back. It will keep coming back.

K-GAR OLLIE: I'm not marching anywhere.

A I JOSH: It's not going to keep coming back, are you crazy? It's here once and then it's gone.

T-MAC SAM: It will come back. It will keep coming back.

K-GAR OLLIE: I've marched my whole life, and then some.

A I JOSH: And then some what? Don't you want to go to America? Don't you remember what Miriam Maker said—

A I JOSH & K-GAR OLLIE: "America is not a country where they can just come and kill you. They can't just come and kill you!"

T-MAC SAM: It will come back. I'll take the next one.

A I JOSH: It will not keep coming back. This is the first, last and next one.

K-GAR OLLIE: How can it take all of us? There are hundreds, hundreds.

A I JOSH: That's why we have to march now. Miriam Maker said—there is law and here there is no law.

T-MAC SAM: A-M-E-R-I-C-A. I wrote it in the mud, on the wall.

K-GAR OLLIE: In America there are doors. I don't want doors.

A I JOSH: What do you mean "doors"? How do you know there are doors? What are doors to you and me?

T-MAC SAM: I'll take the next one. It will keep coming back.

A I JOSH & T-MAC SAM: A-m-e-r-i-c-a!

K-GAR OLLIE: In America there are doors. I don't want doors.

A I JOSH: You two, you two, you two repeat yourselves.

K-GAR OLLIE & T-MAC SAM: You too, you too, you too repeat yourself.

A I JOSH: I've dreamt of this day for two whole years. Ever since I was—

T-MAC SAM: Ever since you were what?

A I JOSH: Twelve years old.

K-GAR OLLIE: I'm two years older than you and I am staying put.

A I JOSH: Two years? What do you mean? I'm sixteen. I thought you were sixteen.

K-GAR OLLIE: I am. You're fourteen.

T-MAC SAM: I'm twelve. I haven't been dreaming of this moment for two whole years.

A I JOSH: I'm sixteen. That makes you twenty.

K-GAR OLLIE: Who says you're sixteen? You're fourteen and I'm sixteen, not twenty.

A I JOSH: I'm sixteen not fourteen as you say I am and you too, you too, you too are sixteen.

T-MAC SAM: I'm twelve.

A I JOSH: The airplane's here. The oldest goes first.

K-GAR OLLIE: Now I have you. If the oldest goes first, and you and I are the same age of sixteen, and Sam at twelve, then there IS no oldest, only the youngest Sam at twelve so no one goes first, we don't march to the plane or march anywhere especially A-M-E-R-I-C-A which can stay in the mud on the wall and never have doors. So there.

A I JOSH: Alright, you're twenty I'm sixteen, Sam is twelve, you go first. Sam second, and I'm last.

T-MAC SAM: That would work nicely, if the plane weren't coming back, which of course it is, so it won't work nicely.

A I JOSH: It will work nicely, oldest, next oldest, next next oldest oldest.

(The sound of an airplane engine)

T-MAC SAM: I wrote it in the mud, on the wall, A-m-e-r-i-c-a.

A I JOSH & K-GAR OLLIE: They can't just come and kill you

A I JOSH: The airplane's really here. Let's march.

K-GAR OLLIE: Does the plane have a door?
I don't want to sleep alone inside some plane behind a door.

A I JOSH: If there's a door, I'll open it. If there isn't, I'll open it anyway. Oldest first—Sam, Ollie, Josh, Josh, Sam, Ollie, Ollie, Josh, Sam, Josh—let's count—one three two, two three one—I'm frightened—

(A ladder drops from the plane door.)

A I JOSH: Just like the Gilo River. The Sudanese Liberation Army/The Sudanese Government which used to be the Liberation Army, they're all chasing us, pushing us hard. We come to a rope ladder to climb up to the bridge, crocodiles below—like stepping stones they look

T-MAC SAM: This is a plane, this is not the Gilo, no crocodiles, no stepping stones, don't step!, no army chasing us, your foot is just your foot.

K-GAR OLLIE: Not my foot—your foot and yours—I declare I'm the oldest and I go first.
I am a GIRL and GIRLS go first

A I JOSH: You're a what?!

T-MAC SAM: You're a what!?

A I JOSH & T-MAC SAM: You're a what? Prove it!

K-GAR OLLIE:
What I have you don't; what you have I don't
Challenge me I'll show; now it's time to go
Never any doubt. I'm a girl and I'm going too and FIRST

A I JOSH & T-MAC SAM: What she has we don't; what we have she doesn't/don't?
O, what the Hey—She's a girl and girls go first. They what?

K-GAR OLLIE:
Hey Hey, I'm going!

A I JOSH & T-MAC SAM:
Hey Hey, we're going!

(They clamber up the rope. And, yes, The girl[s] goes [go] first.)

A I JOSH & T-MAC SAM: She sure is a what!

K-GAR OLLIE: You better believe—I'm a WHAT!

END OF ACT ONE

ACT TWO

Scene One

(You will see you came this far)

(Dream sequence. The Wedding Dance in Camp Kakuma. A Chorus of high-jumping men—very Bill T Jones—hopping, singing, chanting, clapping, shouting, leaping, weeping, howling, ululating.)

(A I JOSH, *in African garb)*

(Nota bene—Nyandier rhymes with "Buy-land-see-air".)

A I JOSH: I want to marry fair Nyandier

(NYANDIER, *an African Princess, appears.)*

A I JOSH: Resplendent in her scent, the air is sweet
With sweat of dancing men who clap and leap
Who chant and sing and hop and ululate
Nyandier in splendid yellow dress, her hair
Done up, a gold stud dots her nose
Her toes, her ankles ringed, it makes me weep
Sweet Nyandier, I plant my flag before your tent
I'll twist and shout, wave and sing
I'll leap and weep and gnash my teeth

(K-GAR OLLIE *and* T-MAC SAM *wake* A I JOSH *from his dream. They are on the plane somewhere over the ocean. Adlibbing, and then—)*

K-GAR OLLIE & T-MAC SAM: Josh Josh!

K-GAR OLLIE: It's O K, it's O K.

A I JOSH: I dreamt we were in Kakuma Camp.

T-MAC SAM: You need some sleep. Tomorrow. First day. This plane lands.

K-GAR OLLIE & T-MAC SAM: We land.

THE THREE: We hope!

A I JOSH: I won't sleep.

K-GAR OLLIE: I will.

T-MAC SAM: I will.

A I JOSH: You're a girl. All this time—

K-GAR OLLIE: A girl all this time.

T-MAC SAM: He means—

K-GAR OLLIE: I know what he means. Now what do we do when we land?

A I JOSH: We hope we land.

K-GAR OLLIE: Do I stay a boy?

T-MAC SAM: Do you stay a boy?

K-GAR OLLIE: They expect a boy. We give them a girl, maybe they send us back.

A I JOSH & T-MAC SAM: They wouldn't.

K-GAR OLLIE: They only want boys!

A I JOSH: I'll never get to sleep.

T-MAC SAM: They wouldn't just send us right back. Look at all—

K-GAR OLLIE: Look at all what?

A I JOSH: I'll sleep if it kills me.

T-MAC SAM: We can't solve this now. Look out the window.

K-GAR OLLIE: I see nothing.

T-MAC SAM: That's not supposed to be what you see.

A I JOSH: I see nothing at the moment.

T-MAC SAM: At the moment.

K-GAR OLLIE: Am I still a What??

(The three, resigned to seeing nothing at the moment, try to sleep as the plane's engines hum about them.)

(Twenty-three hours later, in Fargo, North Dakota, the plane lands.)

(COLD)

A I JOSH: Would someone tell me please
Is it day or is it night?
Are those shadows are those lights

T-MAC SAM: We have landed
And now we're in the State Dakota North
Will we fight like in Sudan, South and North and up and down
Will we war with South Dakota in the country in the town

K-GAR OLLIE: Are the Frenchmen in Pierre like the ones in French Quebec?
The ones we read in Ptolemy Patrick's class

A I JOSH:
It's government, rebels, all the same, it's in the air
Is it day or is it night
The difference, tell me, please, and free me now

THE THREE: And—what—is—cold?

A I JOSH: Far Go, Go Far, North Dakot—to war!
Go Far Far Go, South Dakot—what for

T-MAC SAM: Afrigo

K-GAR OLLIE: Fargica

A I JOSH: Fargica

THE THREE: Afrigo

K-GAR OLLIE: Ahead of us is what we know NOT!
We hope the South is what HOT?
Explain it all to us poor ones
then say it all AGAIN

THE THREE: Does nothing change from night to day
and all remain the same
Will we live inside this darkness still
and who is there to blame?

(They are off the plane and met by Coach ISAIAH MIDNIGHT. *He distributes coats.)*

ISAIAH MIDNIGHT: Welcome to Fargo, Coach Isaiah
Midnight at your beck and call
Coats warm coats for all when the winds do blow
And they do blow across the plains up north
Let's climb into my van and sally forth
Please hurry inside, put on your coats and ride, Sally,
ride

(The three are scrambling to put on coats.)

A I JOSH: Who's Sally Forth?

T-MAC SAM: His American girlfriend, remember we've been warned.

A I JOSH: But now we have a girl and a friend.

T-MAC SAM: A friend and a girl?

K-GAR OLLIE: I wan that red coat, the one with the bull, girls first.

A I JOSH: Not so loud with the girl talk. Alright, you take it.

T-MAC SAM: I'm sitting in the back, not next to Sally.

(They all manage to scramble in ISAIAH MIDNIGHT's *dilapidated van, with* T-MAC SAM *shoved to the back.)*

ISAIAH MIDNIGHT:
This is a pretty nice town, I think you'll find.
The wind blows, the trains rumble—make a heckuva
sound—you learn to like, not to mind.
The folks of Fargo smile, never frown—almost
Our diners are the friendliest around,
excusin' the occasional burnt toast
Ten minutes and we're there
Need anything, just blare

A I JOSH: *(Inside his head)* Who is this—what is this—why am I here

T-MAC SAM: *(Inside his head)* Why am I here—what is this—who is this

K-GAR OLLIE: *(Inside his head)* What is this—who is this—why am I here?

A I JOSH: *(Inside his head)* My heart's so cold, my black lips purple/blue

T-MAC SAM: *(Inside his head)* My neck is so cold, my knees, only my tongue is warm

K-GAR OLLIE: *(Inside his head)* What is cold—why am I cold—why does cold live here?

A I JOSH: *(Inside his head)* I was so eager to rush on that plane.

T-MAC SAM: *(Inside his head)* I must concentrate on my tongue.

K-GAR OLLIE: *(Inside his head)* I must think about this cold.

THE THREE: Kakuma Camp so far away.

A I JOSH: *(Inside his head)* Is he one of those Negroes with the hair like ours we were warned against?

T-MAC SAM: *(Inside his head)* Is he one of those Negroes with the lips like ours we've been warned against?

K-GAR OLLIE: Is he one of those Negroes when you scrape the skin you find he's white?

THE THREE: Why can't Copernicus be with us now, making sense, making peace?

K-GAR OLLIE: Do we maybe see some light over there
Are our eyes so now accustomed to the dark

T-MAC SAM:
Will we ever think of something before this land
Like our elders their cataracts cloud their eyes
Will we ever see an animal who sparkles in the sun

A I JOSH: Will we ever put our heads to the sides of cattle lowing
And rest such rest we lose all sense of hurt
What are we part of now

T-MAC SAM: Do we have a part that's ours

K-GAR OLLIE: Have we ever had a part that's ours

THE THREE: What are we part of now

ISAIAH MIDNIGHT: I'm pullin' us in
So put on a grin
Home Sweet Home is where you at
What cross your path is a big black cat!

(The van screeches to a halt.)

Scene Two

(Aren't you glad you came this far?)

ISAIAH MIDNIGHT:
Yes, Coach Isaiah Midnight, that's me

T-MAC SAM: You're a coach? A coach of what?

ISAIAH MIDNIGHT: I'm Fargo High's anything-with-a-ball Coach and then some.—that's base, basket, foot, tennis, lacrosse, ping and pong, add curling to that.

A I JOSH: Curling?

ISAIAH MIDNIGHT: Two guys chasing a tea kettle sideways with some brooms—it's a real blast—I'm also your most obedient servant from Social Reach. We all need jobs in multiples up here, you'll find out quick, though this here Sos Reach is volunteer, you know, got to keep busy. My motto—Do Not Bask. Multi-task. This is your apartment for the next six weeks.

(They enter the apartment.)

THE THREE: Apartment?

ISAIAH MIDNIGHT: It has running water hot and cold and its faucet never leaks.

THE THREE: Running water.

ISAIAH MIDNIGHT: Here's a bedroom with a door you close to keep the world outside.

K-GAR OLLIE: Door!

ISAIAH MIDNIGHT: Here's a bathroom with a door you close to maintain all your pride.

A I JOSH: Door!

ISAIAH MIDNIGHT: Here's the kitchen with a microwave with a pretty door, refrigerator with doors of two.

T-MAC SAM: Door!

ISAIAH MIDNIGHT: Open it up inside and here's another door for you.

THE THREE: Doors!

ISAIAH MIDNIGHT:
The cabinets with doors hold food you've never seen.
Beans in cans, soup in packs, catsup in a wide-mouth
jar.

A I JOSH: CatsUp, wide mouth jar.

T-MAC SAM: He called himself CatsUp, Jar Jr.?

K-GAR OLLIE: Whaddidhesay?

ISAIAH MIDNIGHT: And tomorrow we'll grill some frankfurters.

A I JOSH: Frankfurters?

ISAIAH MIDNIGHT: Hot dogs?

THE THREE: Dogs?

ISAIAH MIDNIGHT: Hamburgers.

THE THREE: Hamburgers?

ISAIAH MIDNIGHT: You know, from cows?

THE THREE: Cow!

ISAIAH MIDNIGHT: Mayonnaise and mustard/ sour cream potatoes dippin' chips.

A I JOSH: Chips? Cows?

T-MAC SAM: Cow pats?

K-GAR OLLIE: Cow plops?

ISAIAH MIDNIGHT: Cheerios granola bars and salsa spicy dips.

A I JOSH: Dips

T-MAC SAM: Chips

K-GAR OLLIE: Pats

THE THREE: Plops!

ISAIAH MIDNIGHT: Aren't you glad you came this far?
No turning back just turning front.
No turning back this is the hunt.

THE THREE: Hunt!

ISAIAH MIDNIGHT: The clock is set, the radio on, the snooze alarm will wake you from your slumber.
Are there any questions now, 'fore I get back in my Hummer?

THE THREE: Yeah yeah Yeah *(Ad lib questions— "What's a Hummer", et cetera?)*

ISAIAH MIDNIGHT:
O here's the thermostat in case you want more heat.
As Cher and Sonny said, Goes on the Beat!

A I JOSH: Heat, heat.

T-MAC SAM: Sonny who?

K-GAR OLLIE: Goes on the Beat!

ISAIAH MIDNIGHT: If there's anything you want to hear again I'm so glad to repeat.

THE THREE: *(Singing a la Beatles)* Yeah, yeah, yeah

ISAIAH MIDNIGHT: You know The Beatles?

THE THREE: The Who?

ISAIAH MIDNIGHT: Not the Who. O, you're just funnin' me, like Who's on first? The things you guys know!

A I JOSH: What do we know?

T-MAC SAM: And when do we know?

K-GAR OLLIE: And how do we know it?

ISAIAH MIDNIGHT: You guys are a blast, thought you were slow, but you're really fast
I know you'll find this country great
And you three boys will love this state
The first night—the rest of your lives
I'm here to give you your first high fives
You can reach for every star
Aren't you glad you came this far?

THE THREE: Aren't we glad we came this far?

Scene Three

(The beat, the heat, is on)

*(*A I JOSH *and* T-MAC SAM *huddle together on the couch.* K-GAR OLLIE *is feeling around the small apartment, its walls, its floors, its ceilings.)*

K-GAR OLLIE: Therm—o—stat— what is that?
In case we want more heat
He so glad to repeat
We want heat—floor is cold -
Up turn heat—We do what we're told!

*(*K-GAR OLLIE *gleefully cranks up the heat and dives onto the couch where all three huddle together.*
The morning after. The three asleep. Doorbell. No response from the three. Again the doorbell. Again, no response. Pounding on door. Key in lock.)

(Enter ISAIAH MIDNIGHT *and* MOIRA MIDNIGHT, *the high school's placement officer.)*

ISAIAH MIDNIGHT:
Hey, guys! It's scorching, open the windows!
(He looks at the thermostat.)
It's ninety-five! Are you out of your skulls?
(He opens the windows.)
It's boiling, pals, what are you thinking of?

K-GAR OLLIE: Boiling, scorching, out of our skulls, when do we eat?

T-MAC SAM: Finally warm and you let in the cold, when do we eat?

A I JOSH: Ninety-five, what is that, when do we eat?

ISAIAH MIDNIGHT:
Eat, when did you eat? You say, you didn't eat?

MOIRA MIDNIGHT: Isaiah, they don't know how.

THE THREE: When—DO—we—eat!

A I JOSH: I must ask you something, Mister Crispie Tucks—

ISAIAH MIDNIGHT:
Crispie Cremes, you already have—I know—When do you EAT? And why haven't you yet?

MOIRA MIDNIGHT: *(To* ISAIAH MIDNIGHT*)*
Not so fast. We'll work this out.
(To the three)

MOIRA MIDNIGHT: I'm Moira Midnight and I think I know what went down

A I JOSH: Are you here to bring us our food?

THE THREE: Where is it?

ISAIAH MIDNIGHT: Your food is here
And it's clear
You haven't eaten anything,
You sat here huddled all the night
Milk undrunk and out of sight?

THE THREE: Our food is where?

ISAIAH MIDNIGHT:
Right where I showed you, in front of you, please
What's wrong, your eyes, on shelves, on counters, in the fridge
Don't you know how to do anything?

T-MAC SAM:
We see what you point to, but what do we do?

ISAIAH MIDNIGHT: You boys have escaped lions—

THE THREE: Lions fierce—

ISAIAH MIDNIGHT: Marauding guerrillas—

THE THREE: Machinegun-happy doped-up soldiers—

ISAIAH MIDNIGHT: Poisonous snakes—

THE THREE: Deadly adders—

MOIRA MIDNIGHT: They've done all of that.

ISAIAH MIDNIGHT: And you're telling me you do not know how to open a can?

THE THREE &MOIRA MIDNIGHT: Yes! Yes!! YES!!! YES!!!!

ISAIAH MIDNIGHT:
Well, knock me over with a wet noodle.
Welcome to the world of keys and locks
Let's practice openin' this big bad box
Gather 'round, boys
This here's your introduction
To the great American production
Instant food with attitude!

THE THREE: Instant food with attitude!

A I JOSH: Now may we close the window?

T-MAC SAM: And turn up the 'therm.

K-GAR OLLIE: With food in our bellies, coats on our backs
There's nothing on earth we will not lack

*(*ISAIAH MIDNIGHT *starts showing the three "How".* MOIRA MIDNIGHT *takes* K-GAR OLLIE *aside, as* ISAIAH MIDNIGHT *continues to demonstrate.)*

MOIRA MIDNIGHT: Now, young lady, what's this about? And how long you been a 'boy'?

K-GAR OLLIE: I don't know what…

MOIRA MIDNIGHT: Don't lie to me, K-Gar?

K-GAR OLLIE: I won't, I can't, I haven't, I'm not, don't send us back, you can't do that, please, you don't know…

MOIRA MIDNIGHT:
No one's sending anyone back. Just don't lie to me.
I can read. Just this morning online—"Unprecedented

rape and sexual assault of girls in Sudan"
Whose idea? Your mom?

K-GAR OLLIE: Yes, and now she's dead.

MOIRA MIDNIGHT: As you would have been. And you fooled the boys?

K-GAR OLLIE: All the way up to our getting on the plane and then I just said it out loud.

MOIRA MIDNIGHT: And proud.

K-GAR OLLIE: Out loud and proud.

MOIRA MIDNIGHT: As you'll say it to the whole school.

K-GAR OLLIE: I can't say it to everyone. They'll send us, or me, back.

MOIRA MIDNIGHT: You're looking at They and They are not sending anyone back.

Scene Four

(The three in academia)

*(*MOIRA MIDNIGHT *walks the three through the school's entrance. They are quite the curiosity pieces, with students and teachers rubbernecking to see what they are "really" like.* MOIRA MIDNIGHT *addresses the school over the P A system.)*

MOIRA MIDNIGHT: Attention everyone, our newest students have promptly arrived—congratulations are in order to the two boys and one girl from the biggest country in all of Africa, Sudan.
You were expecting three boys, but that was not to be.
I'm sure you'll welcome them with all the generosity
that characterizes our fair school in our fair town
'Though we're at the far end of our fair town
It's fair to say that we're not too far
From the center of things, the center be—

too numerous to enumerate fairly
and fully at the present time
so without farther, or further, ado
Now everyone to your homerooms and make our newest students feel right at homeroom.

(MOLLY MIDNIGHT *enters.)*

MOLLY MIDNIGHT: Mom! I'm sorry I'm late, did I miss the announcement?

MOIRA MIDNIGHT: Molly! You're here now, so come on. Meet A I Josh, T-Mac Sam and K-Gar. This is Molly Midnight, who happens to be my daughter and now a classmate of yours.

(MOLLY MIDNIGHT *and the three shake hands. Greetings. Timidity. Excitement.)*

MOLLY MIDNIGHT: All your names are really cool. A I. T-Mac. K-Gar—all N B A names. But, K-Gar, shouldn't your name be from the W N B A?

THE THREE: W N B A?

MOLLY MIDNIGHT: Like Chamique Holdsclaw or
Tamika Catchings or my personal fave,
DeLisha Milton-Jones. We'll get you the right one.
Your folks must have been really cool.

A I JOSH: *(Eager to please)* Yes! Our folks were cool!

K-GAR OLLIE: Very cool. Very cold. Dead!

MOLLY MIDNIGHT: Oh my gosh. Yes, I know. My mom
told me a little about, well,
What you've been through. Then I insert foot in mouth
you know that expression
the very first time we speak
I make a terrible impression
I'm pleased to meet you and excited you're here.
You hear?
Fargo is fine but kind of a bore.

I just feel like I'm ready, you know?
For something more. I want to spread my wings
'til everyone sings—

*(*MOLLY MIDNIGHT *sings the latest hit tune by a female vocalist.)*

(A BOY *enters, very together.)*

BOY: You sing it, girl, you're the dea ex machina
Bling it on, girl, cello your pa and even yo' yo-yo ma

MOIRA MIDNIGHT: Land sakes o' Goshen, the Kookoorookoo, a Dinka like Youkoo.

KOOKOOROOKOO: Before The Big, I was The Bang
Before The Play, I was the Sway
Before the Ark, I was the Quark

MOIRA MIDNIGHT: He has not at all an inflated id

KOOKOOROOKOO: Sydney Kookoorookoo
Yours truly, El Syd

MOIRA MIDNIGHT: A Dinka precedes you. El Syd came to us from an Episcopal social service. Got his degree right here at Fargo High. Threw his mortar board in the air and felt so free

T-MAC SAM: Ee-piss-co-what?

K-GAR OLLIE: Mortar—

A I JOSH: What?

MOIRA MIDNIGHT: Ran away/ couldn't stay
Now he's back/ A grad come to mentor
Not through the back but the front door

MOLLY MIDNIGHT: He got us all speaking in clean Snoop Doggy Doggerels

KOOKOOROOKOO: It ain't Snoop Dogg
It's Gil Scott-Heron
The Revolution will not be Televised

Listen up kids
I'm into sharin'

MOIRA MIDNIGHT:
I'll leave you three, boy, boy and girl
Girl, boy and boy
Molly and Kookoorookoo, set them to school,
You're in best hands, boy, girl and boy, trey kewl
(She snaps herself out.)

KOOKOOROOKOO:
Good Golly Miss Molly, you got a momma alright
She's nothin' but clear not a cell uptight
Now to the folks at hand
Yes, my Dinkas, your drums'll beat the band
There is the Revolution of one form or others
We all have our versions
We all have our 'drothers
To welcome A I, T-Mac, K-Gar here
As your daddy, Coach Midnight puts it, says so
sublime
You gotta come here with NO FEAR
Ev—er—y Time

MOLLY MIDNIGHT: A one and a two and the Koo know what to do

KOOKOOROOKOO: 'Cause the Revolution will not be
Ti—Vo'd, my brothers and sisters
The Re—Vo will be explo'd
The Re—Vo will not be Blackberried
Long after your ifones be long gone dead lines
After your bluetooths be fallin' out of your deaf ears
You won't be able to re-set or re-wind to cover your
bee-hind
The Re-Vo will not be right back after this message
It will not make your hair brighter your teeth straighter
I'm talking to all those who would start over
or stay the same

or whichever one fits what you're filibusterin from one day to the next
The Re-Vo will report but you will not decide
Because decisions will have been made
And you will not have been consulted
Because you have been consulted ad nauseam
And if you be insulted 'bout what's resulted, know this–
Consensus be over
The drug DRUDGE addicts, the Vulpine news, the
Limbergers will stink to high heavens
and go deaf again, making them deaf and dumb, again
And any Rush to judgment by the Birthers, the
Deathers, the Tenthers,
the TherThers, the "Don't Ask Don't Tell, Don't Breathers",
The Second Amendment, pistol-packing, pea-brained steroided androids
carrying babies into Starbucks
with six-shooters strapped to their sides
aimed right at their 'manliness',
All that will be defeated by a brand-new brand-old strategy called
Reconciliation
And we will have the public option
Because the Re-Vo will not be Intelligent Designed or
Tea Partied
The Re-Vo will not go back to the Palinolithic Age
No jive, one and all, the Re-Vo will be live

(Elaborate male/female bonding gesticulations of a most idiosyncratic order.)

KOOKOOROOKOO: Now, my beauties, a little exercise to see where your minds are
What're the capitals of Mozambique, Chad, Zambia,

Botswana and Burkina Faso, the poorest nation per capita on earth?

THE THREE: Maputo, N'djamena, Lusaka, Gaborone, Ouagadougou.

KOOKOOROOKOO: Wha, Ga—Doog –Goo
I think you'll do, as Mrs Midnight would have it, you'll do quite nicely-nicely.

(Schoolbell rings)

(Enter ISAIAH MIDNIGHT, MOLLY MIDNIGHT*'s father and* MOIRA MIDNIGHT*'s husband.)*

ISAIAH MIDNIGHT:
Look who's back—Mister Kook the Rook

KOOKOOROOKOO: Coach Midnight, yes I'm back and you might say I've seen the error of my ways.

ISAIAH MIDNIGHT: Seen the light, young man? Well, we are a forgiving people; we believe in redemption.

KOOKOOROOKOO: I know you do.

ISAIAH MIDNIGHT: How'd you like to be my assistant coach? That is, if you been working out.

KOOKOOROOKOO: An honor, sir, and yes, I have.

ISAIAH MIDNIGHT: We'll see what you made of out on that floor.

One-on-one, You v. Me, friend

KOOKOOROOKOO: World without end

ISAIAH MIDNIGHT: Amen, cousin. Now what about this group? Any b-ballers here?

*(*MOIRA MIDNIGHT *returns.)*

MOIRA MIDNIGHT: Molly and Koo, and Isaiah too, stop.
The first bell has rung and you all need to go.
Take these boys and girl to their homerooms.
There'll be tests later to see where you place

I think you'll do nicely-nicely, you each have a nice face.

ISAIAH MIDNIGHT: See y'all at practice

MOLLY MIDNIGHT: Me too, Daddy?

ISAIAH MIDNIGHT: You mean I too, Daddy.

MOIRA MIDNIGHT: You want me too, Daddy. You don't want I too, Daddy.

(And they are on their way.)

A I JOSH: *(To himself as he follows after* MOLLY MIDNIGHT*)*
Molly Midnight.
In a yellow dress.
With jewelry, gold and silver, and her hair.
Just like in my dream of Nyandier.

*(*T-MAC SAM *interrupts his reverie.)*

T-MAC SAM: What'd that Koo say? And Molly too?

A I JOSH: What? Molly? When?

T-MAC SAM: Koo. Molly. Then.

K-GAR OLLIE: He was expressing himself.

T-MAC SAM: About what?

A I JOSH: Ree—Vo. Is that Ree Vo Lution?

T-MAC SAM: If it is, that's dangerous.

A I JOSH: Is he an AK47, Kalashnikov-carrying madness maniac?

T-MAC SAM: Does he belong to some front or back with 'Liberation' in its name?

K-GAR OLLIE: Would they let him walk around like that?

T-MAC SAM: Did you understand—

K-GAR OLLIE: Not a word.
Except the "the"s' and the "a"s.

But I will.
It all.
And we better all.
He prepares us for—

A I JOSH & T-MAC SAM: A-M-E-R-I-C-A.

(They all move to the classroom where they take seats among their perhaps about to-be fellow students and try not to look about too much. The cries and whispers, or at least the whispers, begin.)

Scene Five

(The MIDNIGHTs *at home)*

MOIRA MIDNIGHT: Well, that was mighty big of you, Big Man. Assistant Coach? After the lip that boy gave you last time out?

ISAIAH MIDNIGHT: Reminded me a bit of myself. We'll see how long he stays in line.

MOIRA MIDNIGHT: He had to go away for him to come back.

ISAIAH MIDNIGHT: What's that line you always quotin'?

MOIRA MIDNIGHT: You got to go a long way out of your way to come back a short way correct.

ISAIAH MIDNIGHT: Look at that clock, time to retire with your sire,
You still oh so fine

MOIRA MIDNIGHT: Whachu mean "still"?
All ways to you, Isaiah
And just for that I goin' to give you a great big Lay-a CAKE!

Scene Six

(Extra-Curriculars)

T-MAC SAM: I'm in some clanging classroom—like
you'd say—ZOO
And all my past come flooding and pent-up feelings
Make me ice cold
And now I worry to pay the rent
I don't get the 'bought and sold'

Some say, don't bother
I say let the rock be rolled
I'm in this country of the Big Tent
Melting pot—well, break the mold
U S one hundred thousand per cent

K-GAR OLLIE: One who mocks
Me and the way I speak, says that she'll box
Me, kicking speech right off my tongue and yet
When I look at her twice— "You've lost the bet"
Say three or four other girls as she skulks away

(MOLLY MIDNIGHT *is there.)*

MOLLY MIDNIGHT: The boys, the hulks at play, text and
tweet, shuffle their feet,
look at you and shrug—one gives you a hug
So give a little fist-bump back, very Michelle to O

THE THREE: When our classes, finally, are done
We find out there is more.
After school activities?

Called Extra—Core—Ika—Lore???

T-MAC SAM:
For me it's baskets all around and round brown ball
Coach Midnight smiled when he passed me in the hall.

A I JOSH: For me, it's 4-H—health, head, hands, heart—
I have all these things, so I have a good start.

K-GAR OLLIE:
Mrs Midnight said that with my kind face
Community service was my best place.

Scene Seven

*(*K-GAR OLLIE *serving food at the Holy Apostles soup kitchen.)*

K-GAR OLLIE: A scoop of mashed potatoes gravy green
These gray little dots they're really peas
Steam Table Ollie, set before these piles
Who are these folks, what did that old man say?
His color gray, like sick Ayoun, the Lean
He wanted meat, without the fat; the miles
I've come, meals I've not seen in the bush
Days went by, a few gourds and seeds—and who's
This wretched man with these open sores
My god my god, wheelchair, please don't push
That poor person out of the way, his shoes
On backwards—stop this, please open the doors
I can't be in this place, I'll surely die
You must, these doors, please push them open, let me fly.

Scene Eight

*(*A I JOSH *at his 4-H club meeting with a sad-looking American cow.)*

A I JOSH: Ayoun, please help me now, they want me to care for this cow
She cannot yield. Her milk is dry.
I could leave her be, let her die.
I can't help her, look, she's wheezing;
Ayoun, please. Tell me what to do!

*(*AYOUN *appears.)*

AYOUN: A.I. Josh, I come to you from beyond
It's soon this cow will moo no more
But she has one thing left so don't ignore her
Embrace this beast; give your all,
The prize in her eyes is what you'll lead her to win
In memory of me, your Ayoun, don't give her up.

*(*AYOUN *disappears.)*

A I JOSH: Thank you, Ayoun!
This cow is my kith and kin.
This 4-H contest—I'll take her all the way
I am back with my cow and here I shall stay.

Scene Nine

*(*T-MAC SAM *in basketball practice. The Coach* ISAIAH MIDNIGHT *watches from the side.)*

ISAIAH MIDNIGHT: Bunny Shots Bunny Shots
Tie their jocks in knots
Take it to the Hole
Deliver that Rock
Kiss that glass
Pass pass pass
Arms up—Block
Backdoor screen
Point guard mean
Zone defense man to man

T-MAC SAM: *(In the midst of it)*
Take it to the Hole
Take it to the Hole
Sam for the Jam now take it to the Hole
Let that rock do its rotation
I'm The Basketball Man, the Best in the Nation
Since first creation, I am sensation
Cause I'm Sam the man
And I've come to my calling in life

I'm a B-Ball player Extraordinaire, the newest of Air
And I'm leaving behind, behind all strife

(T-MAC SAM *does a very self-congratulatory chant/cheer/dance. He does not feel the others watching him.)*

(ISAIAH MIDNIGHT *blows the whistle.)*

ISAIAH MIDNIGHT: Sam, you forgot to switch, leavin'
your man high and dry without no pick and roll
What you doin', standin' around, scratchin' some itch,
your man be grievin' in the lowpost, without no switch
he ain't goin' to the hole
Grandstandin', chest-bumpin', high-fivin', wiggle-wagging self-congrats-ya-tory
Workin'-on-some-fullbody-all-upanddown-whichway-tattoos
Dass TATTS, my Brother
none other than our
SUPERSTAR?
That who you think you are?
Now stay out the paint
You ain't no LeBron saint
No King James give you the time of day
You think you ever goin' to learn how to play?
YOU DO THIRTY LAPS
WINDSPRINTS AT THAT
WORK THOSE ABS 'TIL THEY FABS
You got to get down that BODY FAT
And be here tomorrow two hours early
for some Real Victorious Purlie
And you better damn well
come in with some FEAR
We don't put up with your cuss, not us
Not here, def not here

(T-MAC SAM, *deflated, starts his wind sprints.)*

Scene Ten

(K-GAR OLLIE in study hall, dressed completely in black. We hear what she's reading and then we're in her thoughts.)

K-GAR OLLIE:
"Seems", Madam? Nay, it is. I know not "seems".
'Tis not alone my inky cloak, good mother,
Nor customary suits of solemn black.
Nor windy suspiration of forced breath
No nor the fruitful river of the eye
Nor the dejected "havior" of the visage
Together with all forms, moods, shapes of grief
That can denote me truly. These indeed seem,
For they are actions that a man might play;
But I have that within which passeth show—
These but the trappings and the suits of woe."
I need no inky cloak, my birthday suit of solemn black
I have no actions that a man might play
I will not wheeze or roll upon my back
I'll find the words, express my thoughts, I'll say,
Apostle's Holy Kitchen, show me how
To live with soup—I must, I think, I do
Is this a revelation, hear me now!
I am the girl who does it. Who are you?

(MOIRA MIDNIGHT arrives.)

MOIRA MIDNIGHT: I want to know about your first day with soup, so to speak, but I also want to know about these Elders who warned you about this country's and people's evils. What did they say to you?

K-GAR OLLIE: They spoke of madness.

MOIRA MIDNIGHT: And that seemed their direst warning?

K-GAR OLLIE: "Seemed, Madam? Nay it was. I know not seemed."

MOIRA MIDNIGHT: Ah, very clever, K-Gar, perhaps you should be a writer. Reading *Hamlet*, are you?

K-GAR OLLIE: Yes.

MOIRA MIDNIGHT: Ah, madness
Do you find it difficult?

K-GAR OLLIE: Madness?

MOIRA MIDNIGHT: Shakespeare

K-GAR OLLIE: No. I like the way the words click and bounce. Rather like our African tongues, wrapping my lips around these bouncings and clickings.
"The Play's the Thing wherein I'll Catch the Conscience of the King."
But I'll never get to play this thing.

MOIRA MIDNIGHT: Why not?

K-GAR OLLIE: Because I'm a girl.

MOIRA MIDNIGHT: I'm going to get you a book on Sarah Bernhardt.

K-GAR OLLIE: Who was she, was she a Lost Girl?

MOIRA MIDNIGHT: In a way. She played Hamlet in the Nineteenth Century. First to do it, I believe. And you can be the first Sudanese.

K-GAR OLLIE: Mrs. Midnight, I'm having a tough time.

MOIRA MIDNIGHT: I know, but never be sorry you're a girl.

K-GAR OLLIE: What can I do? It's how I got here.

MOIRA MIDNIGHT: No, it's not.

K-GAR OLLIE: The Boys got here because they were lost, so to say, and I got here because I pretended to be one of them.

MOIRA MIDNIGHT: You got here because of your ingenuity and your bravery. And never forget it. You are The Lost Girl, but now you've been found.

K-GAR OLLIE: I am she.

MOIRA MIDNIGHT: O, I so love that. Molly says, "Me and Chelsea went to the mall."

K-GAR OLLIE: That doesn't sound right. In Camp Kakuma, if we said that –

MOIRA MIDNIGHT: You would have had your knuckles rapped.

K-GAR OLLIE: Knuckles rapped?

MOIRA MIDNIGHT: Not a good example.

(A bell rings.)

MOIRA MIDNIGHT:
Have to go—come to me later about Holy Apostles.
"Good K-Gar, keep thy nighted color on
And let thine eye look like a friend on Fargo."

*(*MOIRA MIDNIGHT *exits.)*

K-GAR OLLIE: My skin of solemn black, my inky cloak
What do you make of me, you Fargo folk

Scene Eleven

*(*MOLLY MIDNIGHT *and* A I JOSH *enter from opposite direction.)*

MOLLY MIDNIGHT: Hi Hi, A I.

A I JOSH: Hi Hi Moll—I, I mean Moll-ee

MOLLY MIDNIGHT: Did you get your Sosh done? Wasn't it really hard? And that second one?

A I JOSH: Sosh? So-see-o-lowgee? Oh—I didn't do it.

MOLLY MIDNIGHT: Want me to help you? I could help you if you want. Let's sit right down and do it.

(She sits on the ground and motions him down and down he goes.)

A I JOSH: I was doing something else. I have this for you.
(He hands her a sort of necklace.)
It's just on a string. I meant to put it on something else.

MOLLY MIDNIGHT: But what is it?

A I JOSH: It's a heart that's been hardened. From a bird that we ate.

MOLLY MIDNIGHT: You ate the bird but hardened the heart and saved it?
Why—how—did you do that? And won't it decay?

A I JOSH: But then I'd get you another. I'd kill it and eat it—

MOLLY MIDNIGHT: That's enough.
I don't know that I'll want another, but thank you for this. I'll keep it.

*(*MOLLY MIDNIGHT*'s not sure what to make of this.* A I JOSH *is proud of what he's done, but a bit puzzled.)*

Scene Twelve

(One month later —the cook in. T-MAC SAM *and* K-GAR OLLIE.*)*

T-MAC SAM: Got another email from Social Reach.

K-GAR OLLIE: And our cash cards have now expired?

T-MAC SAM: The Super Stop and Shop, The Shopalopalous, will have us turned down at the checkout line. The Family Dollar Store—

K-GAR OLLIE: Ha! —will demand fifty cents to get in the door. Our "Gasolina" card will be spit out and dropped to the cement. I guess that's it, boys and girl.

T-MAC SAM: Welcome to A-m-e-r-i-c-a.

(Enter A I JOSH *and* MOLLY MIDNIGHT. *Ad libs)*

T-MAC SAM: Welcome to the monthly "soiree" of the Sudanese Smoothies.

K-GAR OLLIE: How about Delisha and the Dinka Dolls?

T-MAC SAM: Hey, K-Gar, you ever going to get a date?

K-GAR OLLIE: Or a fig or a newton? What's it to you, Casanova?

T-MAC SAM: Sven Knudsen has been, shall I say, approaching you like madly.

A I JOSH: Casanova Sven? How Delisha.
Follows you to your locker, leers at you as you can't figure out the dials. Offers to help you, what's he say, "May I dial you up?"

(Reactions from all)

K-GAR OLLIE: Stop. Sven's nice. I like him. He likes me.

MOLLY MIDNIGHT: Koo can tell you all about Sven Knudsen.

K-GAR OLLIE: I don't want to know all about Sven.

A I JOSH: Who you suppose Kookoo's bringing to this one. That last one, whoa, Big Fella

T-MAC SAM: That last soiree?

A I JOSH: That last, ah, lady.

T-MAC SAM: And how about Coach Midnight's reaction?

K-GAR OLLIE: I am not going there. Satisfied?

T-MAC SAM: I need to eat—Josh! Molly! What have you brought?

MOLLY MIDNIGHT: Josh and I brought some lentils, rice and onions.

T-MAC SAM: Again?

K-GAR OLLIE: I recall a time not so very long ago when you were thrilled at even the prospect OF!
And now we have a pot. A bit cracked, but not leaking just yet.

A I JOSH: How soon we forget?

MOLLY MIDNIGHT: *(To* T-MAC SAM*)* Once a month—our traditional meal.

A I JOSH: "Our traditional meal" sounds nice when you say it.
(He starts to go toward the bedroom.)

MOLLY MIDNIGHT: I thought we were making it together?

A I JOSH: You and K-Gar can do it. You need the practice.

K-GAR OLLIE: Some gender politics in play here.

*(*A I JOSH *goes to the bedroom.)*

A I JOSH: O K. Sam, assist, no, show the ladies the way of chopping and dicing/very Julia slicing.

*(*A I JOSH *comes out of the bedroom. He is in a bright green robe.)*

K-GAR OLLIE: Josh, you put us all to shame. How did you get such beautiful threads?

A I JOSH: How do you like this color, Molly? I slaved everyday for six weeks straight loading boxes to buy this robe.

K-GAR OLLIE: Which one of the camps you slave in got you this robe?

A I JOSH: Camp Ikea.

MOLLY MIDNIGHT: You wore this for special occasions, like maybe a dance?

A I JOSH: We dressed, well, we didn't exactly dress, maybe for a wedding, leopard skins with our hair dyed red with cow urine—

MOLLY MIDNIGHT: Oooo—

A I JOSH: Well, nothing we wore in the bush, we wore nothing in the bush—

MOLLY MIDNIGHT: You wore nothing in the bush?

A I JOSH: Not nothing exactly. This would be, how do you say it, an acquired taste, this robe.

T-MAC SAM: Too hot. Wear a robe? What's that? Bare chest, some vest

A I JOSH: You like it?

MOLLY MIDNIGHT: Yes, very much. We get very dressed up for dances here.
Has anyone told you about the Prom?

A I JOSH: The Prom? Well I have heard a little bit. It's a sort of dance?

MOLLY MIDNIGHT: It's a sort of dance. To celebrate the end of school. Would you like to go with me?

A I JOSH: Go with you ? As your –

MOLLY MIDNIGHT: As my date. Usually, the boy asks—

A I JOSH: I ask—I would like that, yes. To be your date.

MOLLY MIDNIGHT: Okay then! You have your ceremonial garb already! I'll have to get mine. And then we can go. Together.

A I JOSH: We danced in our village, but this, I think this is a different sort of dance.

MOLLY MIDNIGHT: I think it'll be a different sort of dance for you. Yes. And for me. Different.

A I JOSH: I'd like that.

MOLLY MIDNIGHT: Me too.

*(*MOLLY MIDNIGHT *kisses* A I JOSH *on the cheek.)*

(The doorbell rings.)

(It's KOOKOOROOKOO *and a new person. [Or is she?])* AKINYI SMALLBONES embraces all around.)

KOOKOOROOKOO: This is Akinyi Smallbones, newly from Nairobi. That's Kenya, Molly.

MOLLY MIDNIGHT: I know, Koo. I've been there. Nice to meet you.

AKINYI SMALLBONES: Nice to be met. You've been there? When and how?

KOOKOOROOKOO: What you folks cookin' for Kookoo?

MOLLY MIDNIGHT: I went there last spring with a group of girls and two women chaperones.

KOOKOOROOKOO: "Nice to be met." I'm rememberin' that one.

A I JOSH: Koo outdid himself.

T-MAC SAM: Say that again.

AKINYI SMALLBONES: *(To* MOLLY MIDNIGHT*)* What was the group? By any chance was it WISER?

MOLLY MIDNIGHT & AKINYI SMALLBONES: Women in Secondary Education and Research!

MOLLY MIDNIGHT: That's it. How did you know?

AKINYI SMALLBONES: I worked with them through Nairobi Central Prep.

A I JOSH: Small continent.

KOOKOOROOKOO: The Dark Continent to you, my boy.

MOLLY MIDNIGHT: It was really actually, like, very scary.

T-MAC SAM: The Dark Man's burden.

AKINYI SMALLBONES: Like really actually?

MOLLY MIDNIGHT: We traveled by bus fourteen hours from Nairobi into the savannahs. We were there to help girls write essays and make art projects so they could apply to Central Prep.

AKINYI SMALLBONES: Where they had never applied before. I was one of those reviewing the projects.

MOLLY MIDNIGHT: But the first thing I saw—

(Doorbell. It's MOIRA MIDNIGHT *and* ISAIAH MIDNIGHT.*)*

KOOKOOROOKOO:
Coach and the Missus/ and all around kisses

(Appropriate greetings all around.)

KOOKOOROOKOO: Have you met "nice to be met" Akinyi Smallbones?

MOIRA MIDNIGHT: Yes, we've met. We have an exchange program in the works.

ISAIAH MIDNIGHT: *Enchanté, Madame,* Isaiah Midnight.

*(*ISAIAH MIDNIGHT *with* MOIRA MIDNIGHT *aside)*

ISAIAH MIDNIGHT: Koo outdid himself big time.

MOIRA MIDNIGHT: Ain't that the truth.

ISAIAH MIDNIGHT: After that last one, well—give me a little terrorist fistbump.

*(*MOIRA MIDNIGHT *does.)*

AKINYI SMALLBONES: Molly was just telling us about her scary trip to the savannahs of Kenya.

ISAIAH MIDNIGHT: O, not that again. It's all she could talk about –
The caning and the kids with machetes—

MOIRA MIDNIGHT: Isaiah, let the girl speak.

AKINYI SMALLBONES: I'd like to hear it.

KOOKOOROOKOO: *(To* T-MAC SAM*)* Don't you dig it when Coach gets talked to?

(Small male bonding gesticulation between KOOKOOROOKOO *and* T-MAC SAM*)*

MOLLY MIDNIGHT: Me and my friend

MOIRA MIDNIGHT: My friend and I

MOLLY MIDNIGHT: Whatever—were dropped off by the side of the road

T-MAC SAM: O, those sides of the road—

MOIRA MIDNIGHT: T-Mac?

MOLLY MIDNIGHT: We were told to head down this path, but it wasn't really a path. We walked and walked and finally there was this clearing where a school was supposed to be. And on the ground were all these young children, eight, ten or so, and they were on their stomachs and two "teachers" were going around caning them across the legs and back. The teachers saw us and just went on caning.

K-GAR OLLIE: In Camp Kakuma

T-MAC SAM: There was no caning in camp Kakuma

A I JOSH: No caning

K-GAR OLLIE: There were those times—

AKINYI SMALLBONES: Caning is illegal in Kenya.

KOOKOOROOKOO: Must nota got the memo. You know how these backward countries are with cowhorns, smoke signals, old arthritic carrier pigeons.

MOLLY MIDNIGHT: All the children with machetes

KOOKOOROOKOO: Very different from my time with my foster family. Now they would have got the memo, 'though they do not know that the ReVo will not be Ti-Vo'd.

MOLLY MIDNIGHT: O K, Koo, tell us again about your foster family Knudsen?

KOOKOOROOKOO: They were NICE. So NICE it drove KooKooRooKoo cuckoo, truth be told.

A I JOSH: Tell us the killer hippo story again.

KOOKOOROOKOO: Ah, yes, the Killer Hippo Story! Mister Knudsen says, "So, Koo, are you finding your classes challenging?" And I said "I am a bit bored but I am working hard because I don't want to go back to the killer hippos." And Mrs. Knudsen says, "Tell us all about the killer hippos, Koo." And so I told them how this not very large killer hippo, charged my friend and me. How I climbed up a tree and watched as, below me, this killer hippo just chopped him in half.
And the Knudsens just sat there and said "Well, that's quite a tale, Koo." And Mrs Knudsen said, "It's really wonderful what we can learn from you, Koo." And then one of the twins said, " Ooooh, I know all about hippos, too, Koo! I went with the girl scouts to the National Zoo!" and the other twin said, "Ooooooh, I know even more about hippos, Koo!...

A I JOSH, KOOKOOROOKOO, & T-MAC SAM: I've seen The Lion King fifteen times!

(A I JOSH, T-MAC SAM *engage with* KOOKOOROOKOO. MOLLY MIDNIGHT *joins in.* K-GAR OLLIE *does not. Nor are the adults*—MOIRA MIDNIGHT, ISAIAH MIDNIGHT *and* AKINYI SMALLBONES—*amused.)*

K-GAR OLLIE: Too easy, Koo. Too easy to make fun. And you, Molly, what do you find so funny? These Foster Family souls, they're trying to do the right thing, aren't they?

A I JOSH: Look at what I wear. Seven days extra overtime at camp Arby's to get my robe, my hat, *that* is doing the right thing.

KOOKOOROOKOO: We're in this country and yes, Ollie, there are people trying to do the right thing and yes, Molly, I've been here for three years and I love to sing and dance. And all the while, it's not easy here, not easy—but we're alive.

MOLLY MIDNIGHT: And you're free in the home of the brave.

AKINYI SMALLBONES: And you were brave, Molly, to go into those savannahs and down that path that wasn't a path to see that caning that shouldn't have been.

MOLLY MIDNIGHT: And I felt the heat and the wind and the rain.

AKINYI SMALLBONES:
A long time ago in the life of your ancestors,
your greatgrandmother was in this field of wheat.
The winds blew and bent the strands of wheat so they swayed back and forth.
And then the winds blew ever stronger and the wheat was almost snapped in two.
And your greatgrandmother swayed too,
but she was like the wheat and she did not snap and break.
Then she saw across the plain a rainstorm approaching and, as she ran for cover,
a voice spoke to her and told her to stay put,
and she did,
and the rains washed over her and the wheat,
and many minutes passed,
and she saw through the sheets of water
and her vision was clearer than ever before
and she saw the end of the storm as the last drops passed over her.

A hot wind arose, but gently, and dried her clothes, her body and her hair.
And the wheat too stood tall
And everyone since has stood in that field
And seen the end of the storm and felt the hot gentle wind.

KOOKOOROOKOO: Akinyi Born-Early-In-The-Morning Smallbones—whoever you are, I dig you Dugger duggest. Kookoorookoo back achoo

ALL: *(Variously)* Dig dugger duggest. Kookoorooku back achoo.

KOOKOOROOKOO: And one last, one Lost Thing. The food is all—gone. Now who wants to go to the Kaos and Kakofonay Kafay.

(And, indeed, it is.)

Scene Thirteen

(The K[aos] & K[akofoney] Kafay.)

*(*KOOKOOROOKOO *escorts the boy into the K & K K. Whence Postal Modern Bedlam and Pandemonium reign. Twelve year old kids seated at komputer war games shouting, kicking, whirling around in their swivel chairs, banging the chairs against walls, wailing in delight, squealing in pain, but NEVER getting out of their chairs. The three can only stare.)*

KOOKOOROOKOO: Take a machine!

*(*KOOKOOROOKOO *guides the three in front of three machines, whirls them around in their chairs three times and then "lands" them in front of the screens.* KOOKOOROOKOO *takes a fourth machine. A flurry of lines pour forth from the machines—)*

- The goddess breathes and evermore
- Your building is complete

- Our warriors have engaged the enemy
- Ah, the great outdoors
- May the Lord and Lady Madness, in all its forms, embrace us never ending
- Your building is complete, Lord and Lady
- Our sacred land is being desecrated

(A huge burst of gunfire. Our heroes, subdued and confused at first, slowly, then ever more quickly, dig the mania. Again, the machine voices as the games kick it back.)

- We must act Onward!
- We are pleased to strike
- I am vigilant
- Research finished
- Your building is complete—Madness reigns!
- Our sacred land is being desecrated
- Your building is complete

*(*A I JOSH, K-GAR OLLIE, *and* T-MAC SAM, *having been engulfed by the real mania of warlords, guerillas, killer hippos and more, now embrace the virtual mania of gamerdom.)*

(Again the machine voices)

- We are poised to strike
- I stand ready
- Ah, the great outdoors
- Our warriors have engaged the enemy
- Your building is complete
- The goddess breathes and evermore
- We are poised to strike
- May the Lord and Lady of Decapitation visit your House of Worship
- I stand ready
- Research finished
- Our sacred land is being desecrated
- The Goddess breathes and evermore

- Your building is complete
- The only peace is permanent PRE—HOSTILITY—

(A huger burst of gunfire. The screws turned tighter than tight as vengeful war-cries punch the air.)

(Virtual bloodless war as one last word comes from the machine—)

- Ah, the great outdoors

(As one last burst of paroxysm is about to overtake all, suddenly everything turns very sour and horrors pass over the faces of our heroes.)

Scene Fourteen

(K-GAR OLLIE *and* MOIRA MIDNIGHT)

K-GAR OLLIE: Mrs Midnight, may I speak with you?

MOIRA MIDNIGHT:
Good K-Gar, cast thy nighted color off
And let thine eye look like a friend on Fargo

K-GAR OLLIE: The clouds still hang on me. My nighted color shows?

MOIRA MIDNIGHT: Yes. What is it? Wrestling with Sarah Bernhardt.

K-GAR OLLIE: You didn't tell me that she had lost a leg.

MOIRA MIDNIGHT: That's why I gave you the book. To find that out and other things as well.

K-GAR OLLIE: I found out that the stage is not for me.
I love its artifice and magic light
But something isn't right, I cannot see
As if my eyes are blinded, shuttered tight
Apostle's Holy, well—

MOIRA MIDNIGHT: Not for that either. Alright, we'll help you find something else.

K-GAR OLLIE: No, you won't.

MOIRA MIDNIGHT: I don't understand.

K-GAR OLLIE: My mind has cleared, I see an open path.

MOIRA MIDNIGHT: It's sometimes good to see an open path

K-GAR OLLIE: I'm going back as soon or sooner than I thought.

MOIRA MIDNIGHT: K-Gar, you've spoken of the days of wrath

K-GAR OLLIE: Before peace and gentleness, how you say it, took a bath
There was something I was born to do
All of us born to do, not just one or two
A year has past "like nothing—at its end
You'll wonder why we didn't sooner send you"

MOIRA MIDNIGHT: Please don't tell me you're serious about going back.

K-GAR OLLIE: *(To herself)*
Only to pull me back.
And this time I will pack.

MOIRA MIDNIGHT: You're here because of courage and some very serious luck
Don't press it, K, fate's not a thing you buck.

K-GAR OLLIE: The die is cast
Apostle's Holy did the trick
A man with shoes on backwards needs a helping hand
But not from me
He isn't mine to help
It's Twelve, her shoes with blood that overflows
She can't just pour it in the sand
She's crazed and filthy, comes and goes
I'm hers she's mine I have this obligation

I am her sole relation
I see the end of the storm and feel the hot gentle wind.

Scene Fifteen

(Tableau. MOLLY MIDNIGHT *as* NYANDIER, *that is, in complete African wedding dress.* A I JOSH *in his African garb. He bows. She curtsies. They link arms and promenade to the Prom.)*

(Après The Prom. MOLLY MIDNIGHT *and* A I JOSH *in mid-argument.)*

MOLLY MIDNIGHT:
So you think your love for cows isn't mad
It's not some disease that you shouldn't try
to rid yourself of once and for all—Jeez!

A I JOSH: I'm not saying, Molly, it isn't bad,
in a way, but it's good too, I can't lie
It's where I come from, it's who I am, please

MOLLY MIDNIGHT:
I'm trying to understand, but competing with a cow,
is just not what I've wanted MOST

A I JOSH & MOLLY MIDNIGHT:
I wish I'd never left Sudan/I wish you'd never come to Fargo

A I JOSH: I wish I could go back.

MOLLY MIDNIGHT:
I wish you'd just go back to your cow.

A I JOSH: There's no back to go to. And you can't just make one, despite what K-Gar says.

MOLLY MIDNIGHT: There's always a back to go to—cow SCHMOW!

A I JOSH:
There's no back, there's no front—don't you get it? There's no village, Ayoun is dead.

MOLLY MIDNIGHT: What a terrible thing—in my whole life, I never thought about this.

A I JOSH: It's just about all I think about—and you, I think about you.

MOLLY MIDNIGHT: Thank you. That's sweet. I think about you, too. A lot. Perhaps we shouldn't fight anymore.

A I JOSH: Perhaps—

MOLLY MIDNIGHT: What do you mean "perhaps"—

A I JOSH: I just meant—

MOLLY MIDNIGHT: You just meant to make no demands—
(She kisses him.)
Not quite like your cow, you understand.

A I JOSH: I understand all too well and Ayoun, that's my cow—

MOLLY MIDNIGHT: Yes, I've heard—

A I JOSH: She understands, too.

(Kissing)

Scene Sixteen

(The last supper. Almost. The three)

T-MAC SAM: Next Fall I got a scholarship to—

A I JOSH & K-GAR OLLIE: Lower Southern Polytechnical Evangelical Reformed Christian Academy Junior College in Division Three in the Great State of MissiPPISSI—dass M-I-S-S-I-P-P-I-S-S-I!!!

T-MAC SAM: Don't make fun—DON'T MAKE FUN!!!
Division three—I know what that is
The barrel's bottom—I've read the mags
The scouts' reports, the chances for success
The worth of the degree they might not even give
Disgraceful, coach says
But he also says
"It's a step. Take it. I think there's another
And perhaps another."
Do I miss my life former in the Sudanese bush
Yeah, I can't explain, wrap it around my brain
    but, I sort of do miss that
    that THAT that was that

A I JOSH: I'm going to the Wild West for the last Great Cattle Drive and I'm going to be with the American relatives of Ayoun.

T-MAC SAM: You are out of your tiny itsy bitsy mind.

A I JOSH:
In old cowboy movies, you see no cowboys black
But they were out there in the Wildest of the West
Right there in the front and not in the stage coaches
    back
Back to the time when I leaned on Ayoun
When I studied on the side of that four-legged teacher
When each of us was just one more creature
That's what I want
Not a thing more and especially not more war in store
And you K-Gar? Is it true?

T-MAC SAM: It's true?

A I JOSH & T-MAC SAM: You're going back?

K-GAR OLLIE: To be the prime minister of Southern Sudan.

A I JOSH & T-MAC SAM: *(BIG!)* What?

K-GAR OLLIE: Not exactly.

A I JOSH: Almost?

T-MAC SAM: Sort of?

K-GAR OLLIE: Not at all.

A I JOSH: So?

K-GAR OLLIE: Twelve.

T-MAC SAM: What do you mean, "Twelve"?

K-GAR OLLIE: I mean the crazed radio operator with the battery on her head and the blood in her shoe.

A I JOSH: You going back for her? She wanted me to kill my father.

K-GAR OLLIE: She did awful things, she was a mad dog, driven, diseased.

T-MAC SAM: And she must have died.

K-GAR OLLIE: She may be dead alright.

A I JOSH: And you're going back all the same. There is no back to go to.

K-GAR OLLIE: All the same. I'm going back and if I need to I will make a back
All the sounds of a quiet African night
Could be heard just before a cheetah's bite
I thought of the noises the other morn
As I served up some waffles at Holy Apostles
To the old deaf lady who pushes and jostles
There I was feeding the hungry and lame
And I couldn't I couldn't remember my name
Then out of the mist, I was eight, I was ten,
    came my NAME!
And my name was gone again
    I thought I heard its rhyme
But, no, it's gone forever.
    all melted and lost in the heat of time

THE THREE: Return or not, just as the Elders thought.

A I JOSH: No.

T-MAC SAM: No.

K-GAR OLLIE: Yes.

THE THREE: Perhaps next year we'll think again
Perhaps the pull will be so strong to reunite
But for now
It ought,
It needs
To be— So long

(All on cell phones)

THE THREE:
We all thought we'd meet for one Last Supper
    before we all took off
Yeah it'd be great
    but it's not workin' out
That's the way things shake or do not shake out

A I JOSH: I'm meetin' some budds, we talk cowboy talk
    can't do the dinn
    Yeah, it'd be great

T-MAC SAM:
Can't make the bash. Got bidness of a b-ball nature
    Yeah, it'd be great

K-GAR OLLIE: Got to pack get me back
    Yeah, it'd be great

(AYOUN is with us.)

AYOUN:
Good viewers, whether you've cheered or moo'ed
Hear these words from the cow with the 'Tude
Let's see good fortune in these children's eyes
They could have wept their outcast state
When they had fears that they would cease to be
They could have cursed their mournful fate
Instead they pulled their weight for all to see

And like the lark at break of day arising
Though they could have been despising
They prayed and sang, thus praying twicely—Nicely
  nicely
Now may they sing at Heaven's gate
My crystal ball broke, cracked in some old pot
  with lentils, onions and rice so hot
This much I trust, they're bright and they're good
That's all we can ask for, all that we should
The Lost Girl and Boys of Sudan
Each is now a woman, a man and a man.

END OF PLAY

www.ingramcontent.com/pod-product-compliance
Lightning Source LLC
Chambersburg PA
CBHW052204090426
42741CB00010B/2398
* 9 7 8 0 8 8 1 4 5 4 4 3 7 *